WORLD'S FASTEST ROLLER COASTERS

APEX

BY HUBERT WALKER

WWW.APEXEDITIONS.COM

Apex is distributed by North Star Editions:
sales@northstareditions.com | 888-417-0195

Produced for Apex by Red Line Editorial.

Photographs ©: Iain Masterton/agefotostock/Newscom, cover, 1; Shutterstock Images, 4–5, 6–7, 8–9, 13, 14–15, 18, 20–21, 22–23, 24, 25, 29; Library of Congress, 10–11; A. Loeffler/Library of Congress, 12; iStockphoto, 16–17, 26–27; AP Images, 19

Library of Congress Control Number: 2021918370

ISBN
978-1-63738-172-4 (hardcover)
978-1-63738-208-0 (paperback)
978-1-63738-276-9 (ebook pdf)
978-1-63738-244-8 (hosted ebook)

Printed in the United States of America
Mankato, MN
012022

NOTE TO PARENTS AND EDUCATORS

Apex books are designed to build literacy skills in striving readers. Exciting, high-interest content attracts and holds readers' attention. The text is carefully leveled to allow students to achieve success quickly. Additional features, such as bolded glossary words for difficult terms, help build comprehension.

TABLE OF CONTENTS

CHAPTER 1

BLAZING SPEED

The riders step into their seats. They are ready to ride Formula Rossa. The roller coaster's red train looks like a race car. Soon, it takes off.

Formula Rossa can carry 16 riders at one time.

5

Formula Rossa can go from 0 to 60 miles per hour (0–97 km/h) in just two seconds.

The coaster travels 149 miles per hour (240 km/h). Riders scream as they turn a sharp corner. The train is nearly sideways.

Formula Rossa is in Abu Dhabi, United Arab Emirates.

The red coaster zooms down the track. Riders lift their arms. It is a ride they will never forget.

SAFETY GOGGLES

At high speeds, flying pieces of sand can harm the eyes. So, Formula Rossa riders must wear goggles. That way, nothing can get in their eyes.

Formula Rossa lasts just
1 minute and 32 seconds.

ncouru a l'établissement de la Promenade Aérienne, ils ont ouvert a la frivolité, une Arène qui a vraiment un cou
t de rapidité, que si ces chars étaient trainés par des chevaux vigoureux lancés au grand trot et par un mouvement plu
nt de départ, d'ou ils peuvent encore recommencer leur singulière course faire Quinze lieues à l'heure, c'est a dire voyager
e soit sans nul danger, et que la perfection du mécanisme (que l'œil ne voit point) et la solidité des constructions doi
ont pas privés pour cela du délicieux coup d'œil dont on jouit dans le pavillon élevé sur le sommet de la montagne, car un es
a la vue. Mais s'en l'etendre au loin on peut la reposer agréablement sur la promenade aérienne et sur le jardin qui est dessiné ave
tout et prévu les désirs et les besoins des curieux qui viendront le visiter. Un superbe Café dont les glaces nombreuses multip
dans les salons divins de son joli local, un gauffrier qui mérite d'être visité. Enfin des cabinets, ou le voyageur fatigué
séjour enchanté car un feu brillant, allumé dans le fanal qui couronne le pavillon, éclairant bien de tout cotés remplacera la clarté du jour p

S.t Louis. Martinet Rue du Coq. Gautier, même Rue,   et. Chazal Rue Dauphine N.°35

CHAPTER 2

ROLLER COASTER HISTORY

The first **modern** roller coaster was built in 1817. Riders traveled down a curved hill. They reached speeds of 40 miles per hour (64 km/h).

The first roller coaster was in Paris, France. It was called the Promenades-Aériennes.

monumental
encore, redesc
rant de vélocité
r er la timidité d
x et élégant y co
rcé de charmans
afini la vaste ga
ec sa belle se re
iere vive et pure q

aux mémes adr

FLIP-FLAP RAILWAY

Flip-Flap Railway opened in 1895. This coaster had a loop. It was the first coaster in the United States that turned riders upside down.

Flip-Flap Railway was built in Coney Island, New York.

People can still ride the Coney Island Cyclone.

Roller coasters got faster in the 1900s. The Coney Island Cyclone opened in 1927. It went 60 miles per hour (97 km/h).

The Medusa is one of many roller coasters made from steel. It opened in 2000 in California.

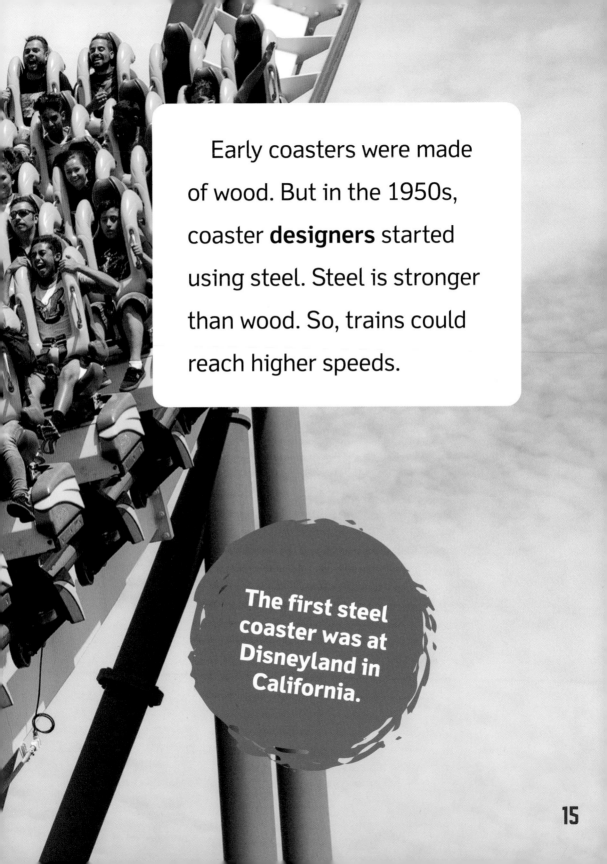

Early coasters were made of wood. But in the 1950s, coaster **designers** started using steel. Steel is stronger than wood. So, trains could reach higher speeds.

The first steel coaster was at Disneyland in California.

CHAPTER 3

POWERED BY GRAVITY

Many roller coasters use chain lifts. A chain slowly pulls the train up a big hill. Then the train zooms downhill because of **gravity**.

Riders go up the chain lift part of a roller coaster.

Tall hills give trains more speed than small hills. So, coaster designers kept making bigger hills.

For many people, drops are the most exciting parts of roller coasters.

The Beast opened in Ohio in 1979. The coaster stands 110 feet (34 m) tall.

The Beast reaches speeds of 65 miles per hour (105 km/h).

Kings Island
THE BEAST
4

STAYING SAFE

Coaster designers make sure riders stay safe. A **ratchet** stops the train from falling backward when it goes uphill. Lap bars and **harnesses** keep riders in their seats during the ride.

Kingda Ka is in New Jersey. In 2021, it was the fastest roller coaster in North America.

Kingda Ka opened in 2005. This coaster stands 456 feet (139 m) tall. Riders go straight down. They reach speeds of 128 miles per hour (206 km/h).

A ride on Kingda Ka lasts 50 seconds.

CHAPTER 4

MAGNETS AND HYDRAULICS

Some newer roller coasters use magnets instead of chain lifts. Powerful magnets launch the train. The train gains speed very quickly.

Red Force in Spain uses magnets. This roller coaster can go 112 miles per hour (180 km/h).

Other coasters use **hydraulics**.
Each coaster's motor has liquid inside.
The liquid causes **pressure** to build up.
That creates a burst of energy. This burst
sends the train down the tracks.

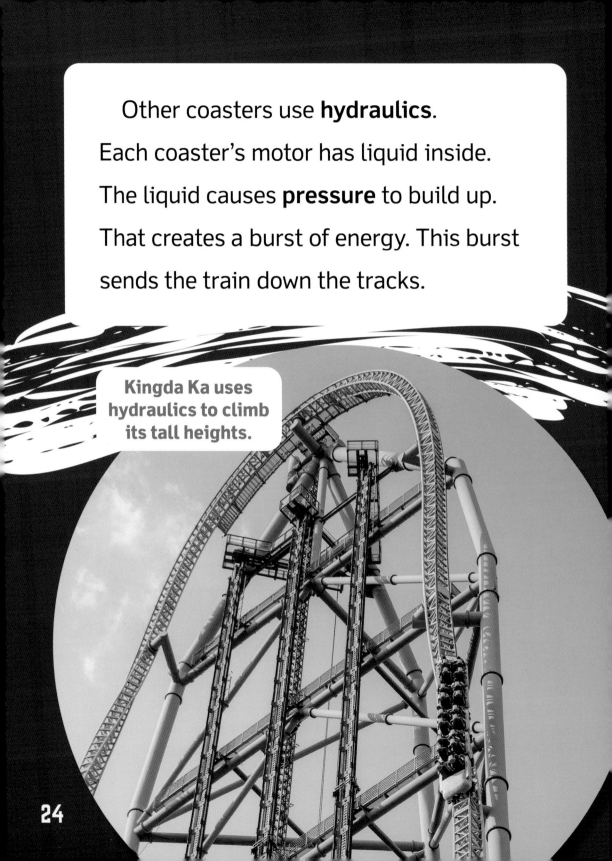

Kingda Ka uses
hydraulics to climb
its tall heights.

Formula Rossa opened in the Ferrari World theme park in 2010. It was the world's fastest roller coaster.

Formula Rossa uses hydraulics. This coaster reaches its top speed in just 4.9 seconds.

The speed of roller coasters is scary for some people. For others, it's the most fun part.

Hydraulic coasters offer smoother rides than magnetic coasters. But hydraulic coasters are more likely to need repairs.

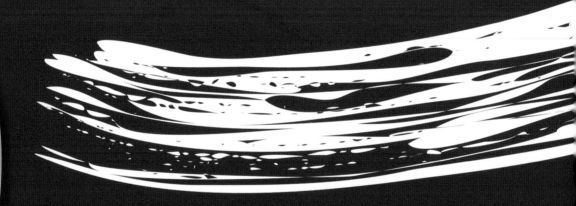

FALCON'S FLIGHT

A coaster called Falcon's Flight was scheduled to open in 2023. Designers said it would reach speeds of 155 miles per hour (250 km/h). That would be a new **record**.

COMPREHENSION QUESTIONS

Write your answers on a separate piece of paper.

1. Write a few sentences explaining the main ideas of Chapter 4.

2. Would you like to work as a roller coaster designer? Why or why not?

3. What material were early roller coasters made from?

    A. metal

    B. steel

    C. wood

4. Why would tall hills help roller coasters go faster?

    A. Taller hills are easier for coasters to move up without chains.

    B. Taller hills let coasters gain more speed from the pull of gravity.

    C. Taller hills can't use hydraulics.

5. What does **sharp** mean in this book?

*Riders scream as they turn a **sharp** corner. The train is nearly sideways.*

    A. having a large group of people
    B. having a loud noise
    C. having a quick change in direction

6. What does **launch** mean in this book?

*Powerful magnets **launch** the train. The train gains speed very quickly.*

    A. to send something forward at a
       high speed
    B. to pull something backward slowly
    C. to stick two things together

Answer key on page 32.

GLOSSARY

designers
People who come up with new ideas for products.

gravity
A force that pulls objects toward planets, stars, and other huge objects.

harnesses
Pieces of gear that hold things in place.

hydraulics
The science of using liquids to create movement or pressure.

modern
Using new and improved ideas and tools.

pressure
A force that pushes up against something.

ratchet
A device that allows something to move in only one direction.

record
The best or fastest performance of all time.

TO LEARN MORE

BOOKS

Allan, John. *On the Tracks*. Minneapolis: Lerner
  Publications, 2021.

Hamilton, S. L. *The World's Fastest Park Rides*.
  Minneapolis: Abdo Publishing, 2021.

Nussbaum, Ben. *Roller Coasters*. Huntington Beach, CA:
  Teacher Created Materials, 2018.

ONLINE RESOURCES

Visit **www.apexeditions.com** to find links and resources
related to this title.

ABOUT THE AUTHOR

Hubert Walker enjoys running, hunting, and going to the
dog park with his best pal. He grew up in Georgia but
moved to Minnesota in 2018. Overall, he loves his new
home, but he's not a fan of the cold winters.

INDEX

Answer Key:
1. Answers will vary; 2. Answers will vary; 3. C; 4. B; 5. C; 6. A